IMAGES OF ENGLAND

ROYAL
LEAMINGTON SPA
REVISITED

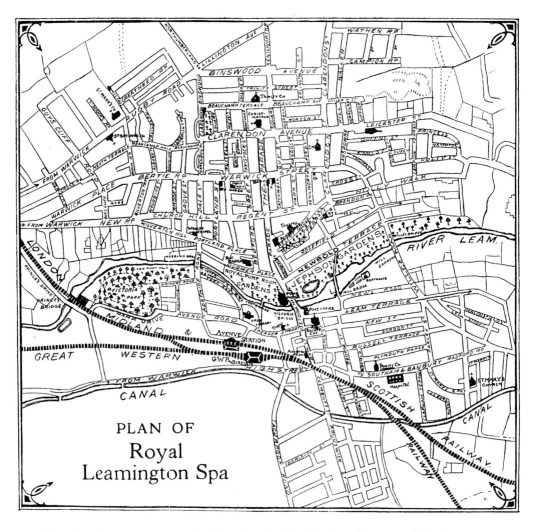

Plan of Royal Leamington Spa taken from the official handbook to the town, published *c.* 1930.

IMAGES OF ENGLAND

ROYAL LEAMINGTON SPA
REVISITED

JEFF WATKIN

TEMPUS

Leamington Spa Tourism and Ticket Office in the Royal Pump Rooms, *c.* 1980. The glamorous model is Lyn Giles, information assistant. Later Lyn, under the married name of Lyn Phillips, became manager of Leamington's Tourist Information Centre. (HEN)

First published 2008

Tempus Publishing
Cirencester Road, Chalford,
Stroud, Gloucestershire, GL6 8PE
www.tempus-publishing.com

Tempus Publishing is an imprint of The History Press

British Library Cataloguing in Publication Data.
A catalogue record for this book is available from the British Library.

ISBN 978 0 7524 4334 8

Typesetting and origination by The History Press
Printed in Great Britain by Ashford Colour Press Ltd

Contents

Acknowledgements

The images of Royal Leamington Spa presented in this book are drawn largely from the collections of Leamington Spa Art Gallery & Museum. Most are taken from photographs or postcards; the remainder are from prints, advertisements and a painting. Many of these items were donated by members of the public but a significant number of the photographs were transferred to the Art Gallery & Museum from the publicity department of its parent body, Leamington Corporation or its successor, Warwick District Council. The latter group of publicity photographs were often used in official guidebooks or other publications, as noted in the captions. When known, the photographic studio, newspaper or photographer is credited at the end of each caption, as is the publisher of postcards reproduced as images. When several images from the same source have been used, abbreviations have been adopted; Bullock Bros, Leamington (BB), Francis Frith & Co. Ltd (FF&C), Walden Hammond, Leamington (WH), *Leamington Spa Courier*/Heart of England Newpapers, Leamington (LSC or HEN), W. A. Lenton, Leamington (WAL), E.E. Lippiatt, Leamington (EEL), Maurice W. Mead, Leamington (MWM), James Valentine & Sons (JV or V&S), and Walter Watson, Leamington (WW). In addition the abbreviation 'HB&S' is visible on a number of the postcards and this too is noted at the end of the caption. Photographs from the *Leamingon Spa Courier*/Heart of England Newspapers Group are published with the permission of Martin Lawson. The writer apologises if any copyrights have been inadvertently infringed. The images were scanned for publication by Tim Crowley, Tom Hitchmough, Vicki Slade and Rozi Smith. Vicki also commented on the text.

The captions are based on the Art Gallery & Museum's records, details from donors, and information from present or former employees of Warwick District Council, especially Dale Best, Lyn Phillips and Pete Rourke. The captions have also drawn on published sources and the work of local history researchers including Lyndon Cave, Bill Gibbons and Alan Griffin. However, the writer bears full responsibility for any inaccuracies in the captions and the Art Gallery & Museum would be pleased to receive any additional information or corrections.

The writer would like to record his debt to the people mentioned above, as well as to the many local residents and colleagues, past and present, who have ensured that these images have been preserved in the collections of the Art Gallery & Museum. All royalties from the sale of this book will be donated to the exhibit purchase fund of Leamington Spa Art Gallery & Museum.

Jeff Watkin
Heritage & Arts Manager
Warwick District Council

Introduction

This book gives a glimpse of Royal Leamington Spa as it developed into the prosperous Warwickshire town of around 50,000 inhabitants we know today. Modern Leamington was largely created during the nineteenth century, when the small agricultural village of Leamington Priors was developed into a fashionable health spa renamed Royal Leamington Spa, and then, from the middle of the century, transformed into a residential town with a growing industrial sector. Leamington's phenomenal expansion in the nineteenth century is evident from the census returns; a population of 315 in 1801 had grown forty times by 1841, reaching 12,812. Fifty years later it was 23,124. Although Leamington declined as a spa resort in the second half of the nineteenth century, it retained the townscape of a fashionable spa including terraces of grand Regency buildings, broad main streets and extensive public gardens. This elegant environment did much to attract new residents and businesses to the town, so ensuring its continued success long after its heyday as a spa was gone.

These images of Leamington should be seen against the wider historical background. The American author Nathaniel Hawthorne, who stayed in the town in the 1850s, observed that from the spa water 'have gushed streets, groves, gardens, mansions, shops and churches and spread themselves along the banks of the little river Leam.' This had been achieved largely through the efforts of a group of investors and developers. The most prominent were local landowners Matthew Wise, Bertie Greatheed and Edward Willes, but they were supported by a network of entrepreneurs drawn by the investment opportunities of the growing town. These included James Bisset, who also helped to attract wealthy visitors by publishing guidebooks and poetry proclaiming the attractions of the new resort. A further group vital to the establishment of Leamington as a health spa was the medical men specialising in 'water cures'. The most prominent, like doctors Amos Middleton, Henry Jephson and John Hitchman, became prosperous and invested much of their new wealth in the growing town. Today a number of these 'spirited speculators' are commemorated in the names of the streets, buildings and public amenities of the town they helped found.

The leading developers recognised that the new resort must offer the elegant surroundings and fashionable social life expected by the wealthy elite who visited to 'take the cure'. At first development was concentrated around the original village, with spa baths, inns, hotels, shops and entertainment facilities erected along the High Street and along newly laid out streets such as Bath Street and Clemens Street. From 1808 there was also expansion north of the Leam, where the 'New Town' was laid out on what had been farmland. A bridge over the Leam connected the original village, which became known as Old Town, to a wide main

Although Leamington peaked as a spa in the 1840s it remained a tourist resort well into the twentieth century. Some of Leamington's principal attractions, which derived from its history as a spa, are shown on this postcard that was probably published in the late 1940s. (V&S)

The Royal Leamington Spa Development Plan published by Leamington Corporation in 1947 saw the town's future as a 'Spa and Inland Health Resort and Conference Centre and a place for residence and light industries'. Here the Mayor, Councillor Oswald Davidson, is showing the local MP, Anthony Eden (right), a model of the proposals. Many of these were not implemented but the report remains a valuable snapshot of Leamington in the years immediately after the Second World War. (LSC)

Queen Elizabeth the Queen Mother visiting
Leamington's Automotive Products factory on
6 November 1958. She is accompanied by the director,
Mr Boughton. Brakes Block 6 is in the background.

street later called the Parade. This had new streets laid out either side, creating a rectangular
grid plan for the New Town in contrast to the more haphazard layout of the Old Town.
Some of the most ambitious and costly schemes, for example proposals to create a series of
huge squares and circuses in the New Town, fell through. However what was achieved in the
first half of the nineteenth century gave Leamington the distinctive look of a spa resort, with
spacious avenues lined with grand Regency terraces and bordered with rows of trees, which
provided a visual link to the public gardens laid out along the banks of the Leam. In the
words of a later guidebook to Leamington, 'the wideness of its streets, the breathing spaces in
its midst which it possesses in the Pump Room Gardens and Jephson Gardens, combine to
make it one of the most desirable health resorts to be found in the country'. The aspirations of
the new resort were reflected in the grand names given to establishments such as the Regent
Hotel, Royal Pump Room and Baths, Copps' Royal Hotel, Parthenon Assembly Rooms and
Royal Music Hall. Above all there was the adoption, following a successful petition to Queen
Victoria in 1838, of the town's splendid new name of Royal Leamington Spa.

In his book *Spas of England and Principal Sea-Bathing Places*, published in 1841,
Dr A.B. Granville described Leamington as 'the king of the English spas of the present day'. A
decade later it had already begun to decline as a spa resort because of the diminishing interest
amongst the nation's elite for 'taking the waters' in Britain. A key factor in this decline was
the spread of the railways, which brought continental spas within easier reach of the elite and
made British seaside resorts accessible to growing numbers of the less well off. One by one
Leamington's spa baths became unprofitable and closed. By the late 1860s only the Royal
Pump Room and Baths was left, saved because the local authority took it over. The survival of
the Royal Pump Room and Baths meant the town was able to continue to provide some spa
treatments while maintaining its long-established role as a centre for hunting and other sports.
From the early twentieth century Leamington also emerged as a centre for motorists touring

'Shakespeare Country'. Even so, its days as a leading inland resort were over and Leamington increasingly acquired a reputation as a residential town. The new, more settled community of middle-class professionals included doctors, teachers, clergymen and a substantial contingent of economically inactive people of 'independent means'. The fact that Leamington itself had been connected to the railway network between 1844 and 1852 also made it an attractive commuter town for businessmen working in nearby Coventry and Birmingham. The numerous large villas built in Leamington in the later Victorian period were for the families and domestic servants of these middle-class residents.

By the 1920s Leamington had an image of shabby middle class gentility, as depicted by John Betjeman in his poem *Death in Leamington*. This did not reflect the whole picture, however. Leamington also developed industries that came to employ large numbers of the working-class inhabitants. This was encouraged by its central location and good transport links, which included the Warwick and Napton Canal in south Leamington, the railways, and the increasingly important network of main roads. The canal permitted the cheap and easy movement of bulk goods, prompting William Flavel to open his Eagle Foundry on its south bank as early as 1833. Flavel's range of kitchen stoves proved popular and the company later acquired the Imperial Foundry on the Old Warwick Road, which was sold to the Ford Motor Co. in 1939. Ford's presence reinforced Leamington's already established role as a centre for companies connected with the motor industry. One of the most important was the Lockheed Hydraulic Brake Co., set up in the former Union Chapel on Clemens Street in 1928. Later, having changed its name to Automotive Products (AP), the company built a factory on Tachbrook Road, and was until recently the largest employer in Leamington. There were also many smaller businesses, including the workshop in Clinton Street owned by the father of Frank Whittle, pioneer of the jet engine.

Since the end of the Second World War Leamington has undergone further important changes. In the immediate post-war years new communities settled in the town, particularly from Poland, Italy and Ireland, and these were later joined by others from Asia and elsewhere. It was also clear by the late 1940s that Stratford-on-Avon, with its tourist industry based upon William Shakespeare, had displaced Leamington as Warwickshire's principal tourist resort. Leamington responded by seeking to develop as 'The Conference Centre in the Heart of England' while continuing to offer good quality shopping and sporting facilities. By the 1980s, when the most recent photographs in this book were taken, there had also been major changes in Leamington's industrial sector, with many of the older established businesses taken over by larger companies. There have since been further radical changes as the present economy based on retail, light industry and information technology emerged. One of the reasons such businesses are attracted to the town is the fact that it still remains 'Leafy Leamington', with a spa heritage of fine public gardens, tree-lined streets and handsome architecture.

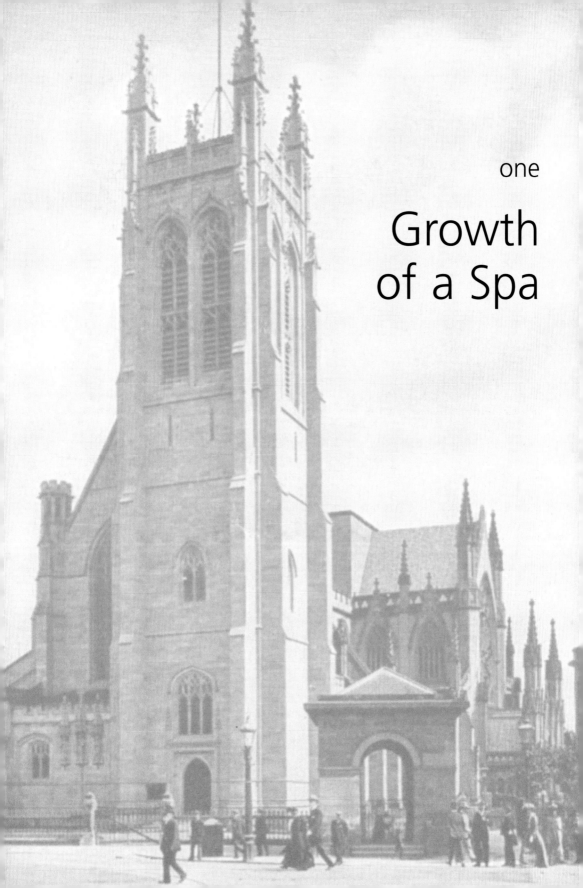

one

Growth
of a Spa

Leamington's emergence as a fashionable spa resort began in 1784, when William Abbotts built a bathhouse over a recently discovered saline spring. Further springs were discovered nearby, and eventually six main sources of spa water were found south of the Leam and one north of the river. Each gave rise to spa baths, which in turn led to the establishment of new hotels, inns and houses to accommodate the visitors. Facilities were also created to entertain them, including assembly rooms, libraries, picture galleries, shops selling luxury goods and landscaped gardens. At first growth was concentrated south of the Leam, in what became known as Old Town, but from 1808 a New Town was laid out north of the river on what had been farmland. Leamington peaked as a spa resort in the mid-nineteenth century but its history as a Regency and early Victorian spa had a profound influence on its later development.

Leamington was mentioned in the Domesday Book (1086) but remained a small agricultural village until it began to develop as a spa in the late eighteenth century. Even after expansion began north of the Leam there were still simple cottages near the parish church in Old Town, as shown in this print dated 1822.

Opposite above: Leamington's rapid growth included development along the High Street, as seen in this print dated 1822. Amongst the new buildings were Copps's Royal Hotel and, beyond the market on the right, Wise's Baths (later known as Curtis's Baths). A quarter of a century after this print was produced the hotel and baths were both demolished in order to lay a new railway line.

Opposite below: The opening of the Royal Pump Room in 1814 was a crucial step in the growth of the new resort. Sited on the north bank of the Leam, it used the only source of spa water found in what became New Town. This print shows the building *c.* 1840, with the recently opened Victoria Pump Room & Baths in the background.

Left: James Bisset (1761–1832) was one of the key figures in the development of the new resort. An enterprising Scotsman who moved to Leamington in 1812, he established a library, newsroom, museum and picture gallery on Clemens Street. In 1819 he built a new museum on High Street, which remained the home of his collection of 'Curiosities From every Quarter of the Globe' until his death. Bisset also promoted the growing spa through verse and in his *Descriptive Guide of Leamington Priors*, first published in 1814. This oil painting by an unknown artist is dated 1793.

Below: An early photograph of Belle Vue Place, the house built by James Bisset in 1817 on the corner of Brunswick Street and Ranelagh Terrace. It later became the Victoria School for infants.

Leamington Church.

Above: All Saints' church was one of the key buildings of the Old Town, and its parish vestry was responsible for local administration until the 1820s. The church itself was medieval in origin and had to be extended several times in the nineteenth century to keep pace with the growing population of the town. This print shows workmen outside the church in the mid-1830s.

Right: The parish church and the adjacent 'original spring', usually known as the Old Well or Lord Aylesford's Well. The west front and bell tower of the church were completed in 1902. This is one of a set of postcards of Leamington published *c.* 1904. (Christian Novels Series)

Parish Church and original Spring, Leamington

15

LEAMINGTON,
UPPER ASSEMBLY ROOMS.
Published by Jn∘ Merridew Warwick 1822.

The Upper Assembly Rooms were opened in 1812, occupying a site on the corner of what became known as the Parade and Regent Street. Including a ballroom and rooms for billiards, cards and reading, the Assembly Rooms were an important step in the development of the New Town. The site was later occupied by Woodward's department store. This print is dated 1822.

Lord Leigh unveiling the statue of Queen Victoria in front of the Town Hall on the Parade, 11 October 1902. The town cherished its connections with the Queen. Leamington Priors' emergence as a major spa town was confirmed when, on 19 June 1838, Queen Victoria granted a charter allowing it to adopt the name Royal Leamington Spa. Victoria had previously visited Leamington as a young princess in 1830 and visited again in 1858. The statue was commissioned following her death in 1901.

By the 1840s the Parade had rows of grand terraced houses, many with their ground floors converted into shops, as seen in this print of the time. Other key buildings in place included Christchurch, closing the view at the top of the Parade, and the prestigious Regent Hotel behind the trees to the right of the picture.

The Parade seen from a similar position as the previous picture but more than half a century later. An important additional feature, indicating the maturing town, is the presence of the new Town Hall, whose clock tower can be seen rising above the trees on the right. This is one of a set of postcards of Leamington published c. 1904. (HB&S)

The Parade's emergence as Leamington's main shopping street is evident in this view from the upper Parade, *c.* 1880. This photograph was taken by Francis Bedford, who may have been amused to include the 'Bedford Stores' sign (top right of picture). At this time the building was occupied by the Burgis & Colbourne department store.

Victoria Terrace, built in 1836-7, was in many ways an extension south of the river of the Parade. The first building on the right is the post office opened in 1870; the railings in the right foreground are at the front of All Saints' church. This is one of a set of postcards of Leamington published *c.* 1910. (JV)

The Royal Pump Rooms and lower Parade, probably photographed from the upper part of the post office *c.* 1930. The luxurious foliage evident helps explain why the town was often promoted as 'Leafy Leamington'.

The river Leam is a major part of Leamington's appeal, lending variety to the public gardens and allowing pleasure boating. Unfortunately it is also liable to flood, as shown in this photograph taken 22/23 May 1932. The Royal Pump Rooms are on the right and the entrance to Jephson Gardens is on the left. The river Leam rose by over 12ft and there were fears Victoria Bridge would collapse. The water reached as far as the Regal Cinema and Adelaide Road, flooding basements in Euston Place. The smell in the flooded properties lingered for weeks.

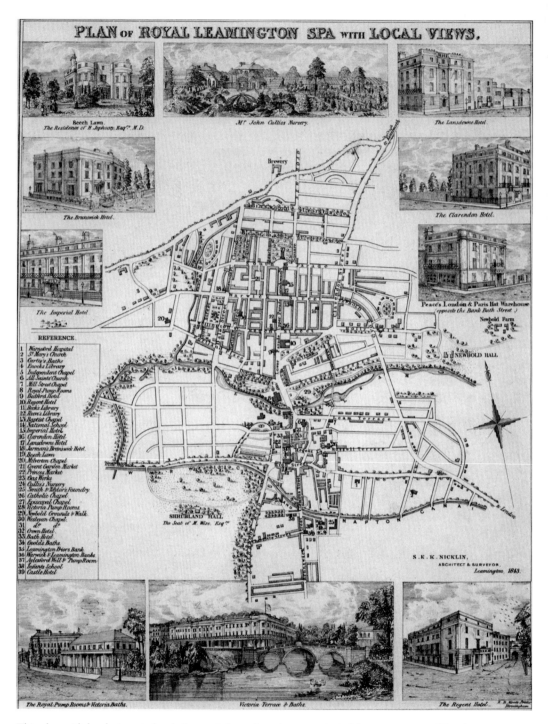

This plan with local views is dated 1843 and shows Leamington at its height as a spa town. The cluster of buildings around All Saints' church (6) is at the centre of the old village; also noticeable is the regular grid plan of the New Town north of the river Leam.

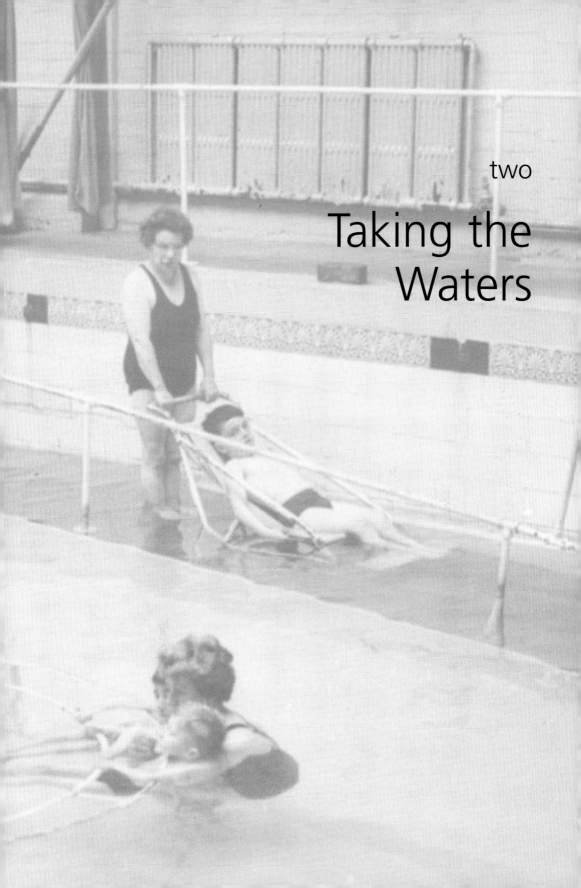

two

Taking the
Waters

Asaline spring by All Saints' church was first recorded in 1480 but commercial exploitation of the spa waters did not begin until a second spring was found by William Abbotts and Ben Satchwell in 1784. The success of the bathhouse opened by Abbotts encouraged further exploration for the spa waters, eventually resulting in the discovery of seven main sources, each giving rise to its own bathing establishment. The most prestigious of these was the Royal Pump Rooms, opened in 1814 over the only spa water source found north of the Leam. The supposed medicinal benefits from 'taking the waters' led to a number of physicians establishing practices in Leamington, notably the celebrated Dr Henry Jephson. The fashion for British spas began to decline around the middle of the nineteenth century, and by the late 1860s only one of Leamington's spa bathing establishments was still in operation. This was the Royal Pump Rooms, which did not finally close its medical facilities until 1997.

The Old Well, or 'Lord Alyesford's Well', was on the site of Leamington's earliest known saline spring. The salty water had long been used to make bread, preserve meat – and immerse folk needing a cure for rabies! The owner of the property, Lord Aylesford, built a well house in 1803 but insisted the poor continue to have free access to the spa waters. This shows a later, rebuilt, version of Lord Aylesford's Well shortly before the shops in front of All Saints' church were demolished in the mid-1890s. (LSC)

Opposite above: Lord Aylesford's Well was demolished around 1960 and the site in front of All Saints' church marked by a stone, seen here being officially unveiled. The inscription states: 'Presented by the National Association of Master Monumental Masons in Conference at Royal Leamington Spa, September 1963'. The marker has since been removed. (MWM)

Opposite below: Curtis's Baths on the corner of High Street and Bath Street seen in a print of *c.* 1846. The building was over a spa water spring found in 1790 on the property of Matthew Wise of nearby Shrubland Hall. Originally called Wise's Baths, they were later enlarged and became known as Curtis's Baths, after Mrs Curtis who managed them. They were closed in 1847 and demolished in 1850 to make way for a new railway line.

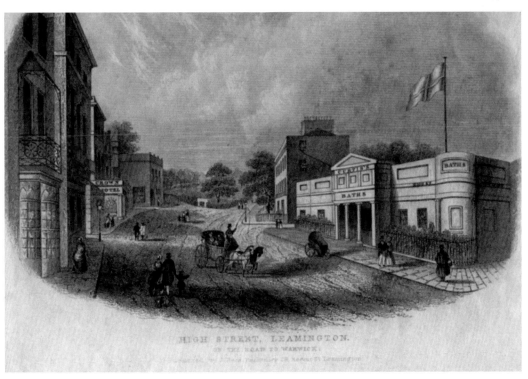

HIGH STREET, LEAMINGTON.
ON THE ROAD TO WARWICK.

Henry Jephson (1798-1878) was Leamington's leading doctor of the nineteenth century. Born in Sutton-in-Ashfield, Nottinghamshire, he trained as a surgeon in London and as a physician in Glasgow. After he settled in Leamington his practice flourished, making him very wealthy. Famous patients included Princess Victoria, the Duchess of Kent, King George IV, Florence Nightingale, W.E. Gladstone and John Ruskin. In 1847 he began to go blind, it was thought through overwork, but continued to support local charities and invest in the town. He built a grand house, Beech Lawn, in Warwick Street and the Jephson Gardens were named in his honour. This print is from a portrait made in 1840.

Royal Baths and Pump Room, Leamington.

The Royal Baths and Pump Room – one of a number of variations on the name of the building now known as the Royal Pump Rooms – opened in July 1814. It was said to have cost £25,000 and contained 'a magnificent suite of baths and spacious pump-room'. A two-horsepower steam engine filled the baths and heated the water, which was drawn from a well beneath the building. The baths on the river side of the building were reserved for the use of ladies and those at the opposite end for gentlemen. Bath chairs like that in the foreground were used 'for the safe and easy conveyance of the bather from the undressing chair into the bath'. Later in the century young Artillery Company officers, after taking their fill of wine at the Regent Hotel, enjoyed racing bath chairs downhill from the top of the Parade! This print is dated 16 May 1843.

Royal Pump Room and Parade, Leamington Spa

Above: The Royal Pump Rooms was remodelled in 1863. Changes included a new roof, central pediment, water tower and different spacing for the columns of the colonnade. A Turkish bath and swimming pool were added at the same time, with a further larger pool opened in 1890. The front was again remodelled around 1950, when the pediment and tower were removed to give the appearance it has today. This postcard was produced *c.* 1910. (JV)

Right: The 'Hammam', part of the Turkish bath in the Royal Pump Rooms, *c.* 1930. The Turkish bath was advertised as 'open daily (Sunday excepted) for Gentlemen from 9 to 6; reserved for Ladies Tuesdays and Fridays all day'. The Hammam now forms part of the local history displays of Leamington Spa Art Gallery & Museum.

The 'Therapeutic Pool' in the Royal Pump Rooms, *c.* 1965. This had been created about fifteen years earlier by adapting the smaller of the building's two swimming pools, often called the 'Ladies Pool'. The buoyancy of the saline water helped support patients while exercising. The swimming pool hall now houses the visual arts displays of Leamington Spa Art Gallery & Museum.

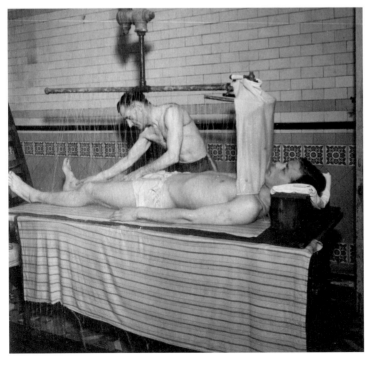

This man is receiving the Vichy Douche treatment in the Royal Pump Rooms. This involved lying on a mattress on a slab in order to be massaged by a spray of warm ordinary water (or spa water if prescribed). It was followed by a warm towel pack and a needle or spray bath. The entire treatment took about twenty minutes and was said to give good results for 'rheumatism, fibrositis, myalgia, and chronic body pains'.

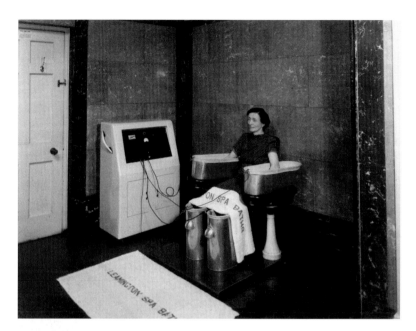

This woman is receiving the 'Schnee Four Cell' treatment in the Royal Pump Rooms. Her arms and legs are in four troughs of saline solution, through which an electric current is passed for twenty minutes. In the 1930s it was used in 'many general, rheumatic, and other conditions', especially those of the hands and feet. A particular advantage was that the patient received the effect of an immersion electric bath without having to undress. (WH)

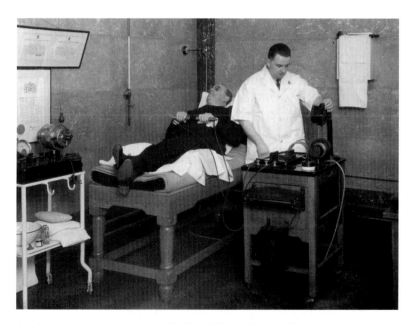

An electrical treatment room in the Royal Pump Rooms. Electrical treatments were introduced around 1900 at the Royal Pump Rooms, supplementing the long-established spa-water cures. (WH)

The 'cooling room' of the Royal Pump Rooms *c.* 1953. The spa water, which was described as a 'gentle laxative and diuretic', was served hot or cold. The member of staff drawing spa water from the fountain behind the counter is probably Mrs Mason. The cooling room was in an annexe added to the Royal Pump Rooms in 1910. (Illustrated)

The staff of the Royal Pump Rooms, 1941. They include Mr Bacon, the Spa manager (sitting in the centre of the second row from the front) with, left of him, Mrs Robertson, the matron.

Right: Dr John Hitchman (1805-67) was born in Chipping Norton, Oxfordshire. A great believer in water cures, he came to Leamington in 1840 to set up a practice in Clemens Street. He opened the Arboretum Hydropathic Establishment on Tachbrook Road in 1863. An associate and friend of Henry Jephson, he is commemorated by the fountain named after him in Jephson Gardens. (Graham & Suter, Leamington)

Below: The Royal Midland Counties Home for Incurables, Tachbrook Road. This was opened by Dr Hitchman in 1863 as the Arboretum to provide hydropathic treatments or water cures. In 1884 it was reopened by Lord Leigh as the Midland Counties Home for Chronic and Incurable Diseases, providing an environment 'calculated to soothe the minds and alleviate the sufferings of those afflicted with incurable disorders.' (P. Parsons, Leamington)

Princess Louise at the Town Hall on the Parade, 26 June 1906. The princess, a daughter of Queen Victoria, was in Leamington for the opening of the Radcliffe Wing of the Royal Midland Counties Home for Incurables. She is being received by the Mayor, Alderman John Bennett, and the escort is the Leamington troop of the Warwickshire Imperial Yeomanry.

The Warwickshire General Bathing Institution and Leamington Hospital was founded in 1832 on the site of the old poorhouse on Radford Road. It was later renamed the Warneford Hospital, after one of its most generous benefactors, the Reverend Samuel Warneford (1763-1855). This print shows the original building providing fifty beds. It was subsequently extended several times, having an Infirmary with 120 beds by the early twentieth century. The hospital closed in the early 1990s and the site redeveloped for housing.

three

The Sporting Life

From the early nineteenth century, Leamington's May to October season for 'taking the waters' was complemented by a winter 'hunting season'. Wealthy sportsmen stayed in local hotels or rented houses to ride with the foxhunt or to attend horse races nearby. As more public gardens and parks were laid out in Leamington, these too attracted sporting events. By the 1830s, archery tournaments were being held in the town, which later also became a venue for croquet, cricket, real (or 'royal') tennis, and lawn tennis. Other important tournaments held in Leamington included fencing and bowls. By the twentieth century, while Leamington was no longer a leading spa resort, it still offered high quality indoors and outdoors sports facilities.

The hunt meeting on the Pump Room Gardens, *c.* 1954. Leamington's Mayor, Councillor Edwin Fryer, is shaking hands with a horse rider. In the early twentieth century it was claimed in *The Field* that 'The hunting man views Leamington as a sort of Paradise on earth, as social club life can be enjoyed there, and he can hunt six days a week with the choice of seven packs of hounds'. Social life for riders was lively during the winter hunting season but much quieter in summer, when many of the large houses were locked up. (LSC)

Opposite above: Ladies in Jephson Gardens using the traditional longbow to shoot at targets, seen in a print dated 1 August 1857. Archery, which was popular with both sexes, had taken place since 1834 on what later became the Jephson Gardens. In June 1851 Leamington hosted the first Leamington & Midland Counties Archery Meeting, which became an annual event.

Opposite below: Archers at Trinity School, Guys Cliffe Avenue. This was the base of the Royal Leamington Spa Archery Society from the mid-1970s until 1992-93. The archers are using modern bows, which are more powerful than the traditional longbow. This photograph is stamped 16 October 1978.

Archery Ground Jephson Gardens, Leamington

Playing croquet by the lakeside in Jephson Gardens, *c.* 1870. The gardens were a venue for croquet from the 1860s, when a shed was used to store the equipment. In 1874 the first Leamington and Midland Counties croquet tournament was held in Jephson Gardens. (F. Bedford)

Playing lawn tennis on the grass courts in Victoria Park, *c.* 1922. There were also grass courts in the Jephson Gardens that were used for an open tournament held each July. Both venues also had hard courts by the 1930s. (FF&C)

Leamington College for Girls' tennis team, 1932 – 33. Front row, left to right: Berthe Corbett, Gladys Hull, Deb Farmer; back row, left to right: Mollie Pugh, Jean Whitehead, Frankie Moon. Judging by the presence of the Town Hall clock tower in the background, the photograph for this postcard was taken in Victoria Park.

Modern lawn tennis is often said to have been founded in Leamington. Its centenary was celebrated in June 1972 with the installation of this floral design around the clock in Jephson Gardens. It commemorated Major Thomas Henry ('Harry') Gem, a solicitor, and his friend Batista Periera, a Spanish merchant, playing what they at first called 'pelota' on the lawns of the Manor House Hotel.

Men playing bowls on Victoria Park. The Royal Leamington Spa Bowling Club was formed around 1909, with its original green at Victoria Park Lodge, Avenue Road. By the 1960s bowls was being described in Leamington's official guidebook as the town's predominant game.

Ladies Bowls Tournament in Victoria Park, 1954. Since 1974 Victoria Park has hosted the English Women's Bowling Association's National Championship. It also has the unique distinction of hosting two Women's World Bowls Championships, one in 1996 and the other in 2004. (LSC)

Above: Fencing tournament in the assembly room of the Town Hall on the Parade. This photograph may have been taken during one of the Leamington Easter Tournaments, first held in 1934. The tournament continued to take place in Leamington until it was moved to Birmingham University in 1975.

Right: Posing by the diving boards of the smaller swimming pool in the Royal Pump Rooms. The pool was built around 1863 and became known as the 'Ladies Pool' because for many years its use was reserved for women and children. It was converted into the Therapeutic Pool in around 1950.

Above: Swimming contest in the large pool in the Royal Pump Rooms. The pool, 100ft long and 40ft wide, was designed by Leamington's Borough engineer and surveyor, William de Normanville, and opened in 1890. At first it was only for use by men but later mixed bathing was permitted. The swimming pool hall now houses Leamington Library. (LSC)

Anthony Eden opening the refurbished large swimming pool in the Royal Pump Rooms,
27 October 1956. At the time Eden was Prime Minister and MP for Warwick and Leamington. (LSC)

Demonstrating Kabbadi, a team sport originally from South Asia, in the Pump Room Gardens.
This photograph is stamped 16 October 1978.

Opposite below: Group from King's High School for Girls, Warwick, by the large swimming pool,
March 1949. Those standing include 'Val' Clarke (left), Daphne Wilkinson (fourth from left), and
Norris Harrison (right). Harry Barnett is crouching in the centre. Many local school children
learnt to swim in the Royal Pump Rooms. (LSC)

Leamington-born Randolph Turpin (1928-66) became World Middleweight Boxing Champion after defeating Sugar Ray Robinson in 1951. He is shown here on the balcony of Leamington's Town Hall at a civic reception held for him following his triumph. A statue of Randolph Turpin was erected in Warwick's Market Place in 2001, fifty years after his victory over Robinson. (Graphic Photo Union, London)

four

Jephson
Gardens

Jephson Gardens, extending over 13 acres of the north bank of the river Leam, were created as Leamington was beginning to fade as a spa resort. Laid out on land provided by Edward Willes and named in honour of Dr Henry Jephson, they were opened with great ceremony on 12 May 1846. The gardens were managed by trustees until 1896, when they were transferred by Act of Parliament to the Leamington Corporation. Town guidebooks of the 1930s claimed they were 'among the most beautiful ornamental public gardens in the country.' For many years admission on weekdays was 1d and free at weekends. Free admission throughout the week was finally introduced in 1971 because it was not economically viable to convert the turnstiles to the new decimal coinage. A variety of sporting events and entertainments took place in the gardens, notably the Lights of Leamington, held each summer from 1951 to 1961.

The lodges either side of the main entrance from the Parade into Jephson Gardens, c. 1930. They were erected in 1846, the same year that the gardens were opened. Their height was restricted to 30 ft so that they did not appear out of scale with their surroundings. The fountains visible in the lake in the background are based on one in Hampton Court and were installed in 1925-26. Note the banner advertising the band of the King's Royal Irish Hussars – one of many military bands which have played in Jephson Gardens over the years. (WH)

Opposite above: The Willes Road entrance to Jephson Gardens, c. 1900. The East Lodge, erected in 1847, is just visible inside the gates. (FF&C)

Opposite below: The Hitchman Fountain with the Royal Pump Rooms in the background, c. 1930. This large, ornate fountain was unveiled on 28 October 1869 in memory of Dr John Hitchman, an associate and friend of Dr Henry Jephson. (WH)

The Jephson Memorial, unveiled 28 May 1849. This was funded by residents who wanted to create a 'striking public testimonial' to Leamington's most celebrated physician. The Corinthian temple-style building is of Bath stone and the marble statue of Dr Jephson is by the Birmingham sculptor Peter Hollins. This photograph was used in a postcard published in 1960.

Above: The obelisk in the centre of this photograph commemorates Edward Willes of Newbold Comyn, who provided the land for Jephson Gardens. It was erected by the gardens' trustees in 1875 to placate Edward's son William, who felt his father's generosity should be better acknowledged. This photograph seems to have been taken around 1960. (LSC)

Right: The Davis Clock Tower after a snowfall. Erected in 1925, this was funded anonymously and dedicated the following year to the memory of William Davis, a former councillor, alderman and mayor of Leamington. The clock chimes were silenced in 1933 to avoid disturbing local residents, but were reinstated in 1986.

The Promenade Cafeteria was open during summer for light refreshments and cold snacks. The top of the domed roof of the nearby Pavilion Theatre is just visible in the background. The cafeteria was demolished after the extensive floods of Easter 1998. This photograph was used in the official guidebooks to Leamington published in the 1960s. (LSC)

Woodland Walks were created in Jephson Gardens for visitors to enjoy healthy strolls. The building to the right of the paths is the back of the refreshment arbour. This postcard was postmarked in 1905. (WAL)

Anthony Eden, then MP for Leamington and Warwick, ceremonially planting a tree in Jephson
Gardens, 1953. On the right of the picture is Councillor Edwin Fryer, Mayor of Leamington.
(LSC)

'Many thousand fairy lights' – candles in coloured glass jars – were strung out across the lake in
Jephson Gardens as part of the Illuminations introduced in the summer of 1889. There were also
mid-week promenade concerts held from 8 p.m. to 10 p.m. in the electrically lit bandstand. The
summer illuminations were put on for two decades or more – this postcard was postmarked in
1908. (Peacock Brand)

Summer illuminations in Jephson Gardens were revived in 1951 as Leamington's main contribution to the Festival of Britain. The 'Illuminated Pleasure Gardens' created were so successful that the Lights of Leamington festival was held from July to October for the next ten years. This postcard shows the Parade entrance into the Lights of Leamington in 1955.

The 'Main Flower Beds' of the Lights of Leamington seen in a postcard. The lights were electric rather than the candles in glass jars used at the beginning of the twentieth century.

The beer tent of Mitchells & Butlers Ltd, the well-known Midlands brewers. The souvenir booklet for the Lights of Leamington 1958 mentions 'The Jephson Tavern, at one end of the Riverside beer garden where thousands of lamps and lanterns spread their gaiety'. (MWM)

The events organised as part of the Lights of Leamington included a band playing on a float moored on the lake. The float was decorated in various styles, including the Chinese pagoda seen here.

The Lights of Leamington offered 'many tableaux to delight the youngsters' such as this Guinness time piece. Beneath the clock is a toucan, the bird that became a symbol of the famous beer. Other animals used in Guinness' advertising at this time included the kangaroo, seal and bear visible in the model caravan to the right. This photograph was reproduced as a postcard in 1961. (MWM)

Corporation parks' staff installing the Lights of Leamington. The festival attracted over 300,000 visitors each year, including coach parties from all over the country. The cost of staging the event, the wear of so many visitors on the gardens, parking problems and late-night rowdiness meant that the Lights were discontinued after the 1961 season.

five

Parks and Gardens and Shady Walks

The importance of green open spaces for visitors coming to 'take the waters' was recognised from the early days of the spa resort. Many of Leamington's pump rooms and baths, including the Royal Pump Rooms, had their own private gardens. There were also pleasure gardens like those laid out in the Old Town in 1811, later known as Ranelagh Gardens, or in the 1830s on the north bank of the Leam, on land later incorporated into Jephson Gardens. At first these were largely reserved for patrons and subscribers but as Leamington grew there was an increasing need to provide outdoors recreational spaces for all the local community. The local authority took the lead, creating a number of riverside walks, opening the Pump Room Gardens to the public, and, as seen in the previous chapter, taking over the management of Jephson Gardens. *The Red Guide to Leamington* observed in the 1930s that 'parks and gardens and shady walks so abound that from Willes Bridge on the east to the waterfall at the end of the New River Walk it is possible to stroll for a mile without leaving the verdure of grass and trees'. In the 1960s this chain of open spaces was extended eastwards as far as Newbold Comyn and westwards to the Edmondscote Sports Track.

Linden Avenue in Pump Room Gardens was first planted in 1828, 'forming one of the finest promenades in the garden town'. In 1875 the Avenue was opened to the general public, followed fourteen years later by the rest of the Pump Room Gardens. This image is taken from a set of postcards of Leamington published *c.* 1904. (HB&S)

Opposite above: Band playing in the bandstand in Pump Room Gardens, with the tower of St Peter's church in the background. Bands were a regular attraction on summer Sunday afternoons in Leamington's public gardens. Taken from a set of postcards of Leamington published *c.* 1904. (HB&S)

Pump Room Gardens. Leamington. H.B&S.

Below: Rustic wooden footbridge crossing the entrance from the river Leam to the boating lake in Mill Gardens. The Mill Gardens were opened in January 1903. They were laid out on the south bank of the Leam, using land released by the demolition of Oldham's Mill. The bandstand and Pavilion visible on the other side of the river opened shortly before this postcard was published around 1910. (JV)

Mill Gardens, Leamington Spa.

This boathouse was built for the lake created in Mill Gardens. It housed the rowing boats, canoes and punts available for hire. This postcard was published around 1910.

The weir and bridge were designed by William de Normanville, Leamington's Borough engineer and surveyor. The weir was part of a scheme to improve the flow of the Leam by widening the channel. A water-driven turbine inside the weir was used to pump water from the river to a reservoir on the Campion Hills. Taken from a set of postcards of Leamington published *c.* 1904. (HB&S)

Willes Road Bridge seen from Mill Gardens. The two canoes in the foreground were presumably hired from the Mill Gardens boathouse. When first built in 1827 the bridge was known as Newbold Bridge and formed part of Newbold Road. The bridge was renovated in 1876, at about the same time that the name of the road and bridge was changed to Willes, in honour of the family that provided the land for Jephson Gardens. This postcard was published around 1910. (JV)

View from William de Normanville's suspension bridge over the weir. The horse is standing on the stone-paved slipway used for watering and washing horses. It was constructed around 1880 to replace an earlier watering place closer to the Victoria Bridge, seen downstream. Reputedly both slipways were also used for washing circus elephants, giving rise to the name Elephant Walk. One of a set of postcards of Leamington published c. 1904. (HB&S)

The 'strip garden' between Hamilton Terrace and Regent Grove. The cannon visible in the middle of the picture was captured at the siege of Sebastapol during the Crimean War. It was given to Leamington as a trophy in July 1857, being placed in Jephson Gardens before it was moved to Holly Walk.

The New River Walk, *c.* 1870. New River Walk runs by the side of the Leam from Adelaide Road Bridge to the weir by Princes Drive. It was opened in1862, having been created in the course of improvements to straighten the river, so speeding the flow of sewage away from the town. The land adjoining New River Walk was laid out as Victoria Park in 1897. (Francis Bedford)

New River Walk with Adelaide Road Bridge in the background, *c.* 1890. The stone bridge shown here was thought to be unsafe for heavy traffic and replaced by an iron one in 1891. (Graham's Art Studio)

ADELAIDE BRIDGE, LEAMINGTON.

Adelaide Road Bridge after it was rebuilt in iron to a design by William de Normanville. The new bridge opened in August 1891; this postcard shows it around 1910. (Dainty Series)

York Walk seen from Adelaide Road Bridge. Opened in July 1893, it was named after the Duke of York, who had just married Princess May of Teck. The couple later became King George V and Queen Mary. York Walk was designed by William de Normanville and laid out on ground formerly belonging to the Victoria Nursery. This postcard was postmarked 29 August 1904. (Stengel & Co., London)

This redundant steamroller was placed in Victoria Park for children to play on. It was removed around 1990 because it could not be made to comply with increasingly stringent health and safety legislation. The park was opened and named to mark Queen Victoria's Diamond Jubilee in 1897.

This climbing frame in Victoria Park's play area was shaped like a 1960s space capsule. It had to be removed because, like the steamroller in the previous picture, it could not be made to comply with current health and safety legislation.

The Dell, off Warwick Place, is one of Leamington's smaller public gardens. It is some distance from the main chain of parks and gardens along the Leam. (LSC)

Centre Tree of England H.B.S.

Above: The Midland Oak was claimed to mark the centre of England. The importance attached to it is indicated by the protective fence visible in this postcard published around 1904. The ancient tree shown here was felled in 1967 as being in a dangerous condition. A new oak, a descendant of the original, was planted in 1988. (HB&S)

Left: Often described as 'Leafy Leamington' or 'the garden town of the Midlands', Leamington has won many prizes in the Britain in Bloom competition. Here Mary Cridlan, chairman of the Leamington in Bloom Committee, and Alan Pedley, amenities officer for Warwick District Council, are receiving the Heart of England Trophy for Best Large Town from Viscountess Cobham in 1987.

six

That's
Entertainment!

Wealthy visitors attended spa resorts not only for health treatments but also to enjoy the entertainments that were an important part of fashionable social life. In Leamington this involved balls, concerts and social gatherings in the assembly rooms, military-style bands in the gardens, and plays and musicals in various venues. After the mid-nineteenth century, as Leamington began to change from a resort into a residential town, it became home to a number of theatres, concert halls, cinemas and other venues which increasingly catered for the local community rather than the diminishing number of tourists.

The orchestra is playing in the bandstand erected in 1850 in Jephson Gardens. It was replaced around 1880 with a larger bandstand. The archery targets visible in the background are a reminder that the Jephson Gardens were also an important venue for sports. This print is dated 8 September 1860.

Opposite above: Postcard showing the opening of the New Bandstand in Jephson Gardens, 27 May 1909. This was sited by the Leam and replaced the earlier bandstand near Newbold Terrace, which had provoked complaints from residents about the loud music. Mr R.E.L. Naylor of Harrington House, one of the nearest residents to the earlier bandstand, joined with Alderman Alfred Holt to fund the New Bandstand.

Below: This group of ladies are in the New Bandstand after its open seating area had been enclosed and roofed, to create what became known variously as the New Bandstand and Pavilion, the Jephson Gardens Pavilion or the Pavilion Theatre. Seating up to 1,000, this was used for concerts, operas, musicals, variety shows, ballets, conferences, wrestling and boxing matches. It was demolished in 1973.

Dancers in the New Bandstand and Pavilion during the Second World War. Between 1940 and 1942 the Free Czechoslovak Army was based in Warwickshire, with its headquarters in Harrington House, Leamington. Various events were organised to show Czechoslovak culture to the local residents and to provide entertainment for the Czechoslovak troops. (Czechoslovak Army Film & Photo Service)

Swan Lake in Jephson Gardens! This looks like a publicity photograph taken in the 1950s for one of the Lights of Leamington's open-air ballets or for a ballet in the New Bandstand and Pavilion. (MWM)

Band playing in front of the Promenade Cafeteria in Jephson Gardens. The bridge in Mill Gardens can be seen on the other bank of the river. This photograph is stamped 10 October 1963. (Royal Pump Rooms)

Dale Best in front of the Royal Spa Centre, which replaced the New Bandstand and Pavilion. Built on the site of Harrington House, Newbold Terrace, the Royal Spa Centre was opened on 15 June 1972 by Anthony Eden, then Earl of Avon. This photograph was taken on 16 May 1979 – two days after Dale took up the post of deputy amenities officer for Warwick District Council. (HEN)

Leamington Male Voice Choir.

Artistes:

Miss Marie Stuart.
Mr. Ben Davies.

Solo Violin:

Mr. Geoffrey Gibbs.

Accompanists:

Miss Florence Dudley.
The Honourable Henry Fowler.

Hon. Conductor:

Mr. A. E. Gibbs, Mus. Bac.

The Choir.

Messrs.	E. Ainsworth	Messrs.	W. G. Meredith
	J. E. Bulley		B. Morris
	W. H. Buckley		A. Owens
	J. S. Bywater		T. H. Perry
	J. Chizketts		C. E. Phillips
	F. H. Clarke		H. W. Prestidge
	J. W. C. Corbett		B. Pressey
	E. S. Curwen		G. Rench
	C. Davis		W. H. Robinson
	H. T. Dawson		P. S. Shepherd
	W. Devison		W. Shirley
	J. Duggins		H. P. Smith
	J. Ferguson		W. S. Spurr
	C. Gold		W. H. Stamps
	E. E. Grason		G. P. Stubbs
	A. E. Greenfield		W. L. Stubbs
	J. Gazzison		J. Tarplee
	H. R. Horswill		B. H. Thorp
	F. C. Humphries		W. P. Williams
	E. A. Mann		W. T. Wootton
	G. Mason		

Above: The Town Hall, opened on the Parade in 1884, had rooms available for a variety of entertainments including balls, dances, concerts and recitals. This is the main assembly room, seen according to a note on the photograph 'previous to alterations in July 1934'.

Left: Leamington Male Voice Choir sang in the Town Hall on Saturday 9 April 1910, starting at 3 p.m. This page from the published programme lists the names of the choir and shows the two lead 'artistes'.

Since the Royal Pump Rooms opened in 1814 its main assembly room has been one of Leamington's principal amenities. The town's official guidebook published around 1930 reproduced this photograph of the assembly room or 'Tea Lounge', promising 'the daintiest fare in most comfortable and artistic surroundings, whilst listening to a Ladies Orchestra … Balcony teas are also obtainable.' (WH)

The Lesley Clay Trio in the main assembly room in the Royal Pump Rooms, *c.* 1960. The trio were regular performers in the assembly room – often advertised as the 'Tea Room' – around this time.

A ball in Regency costume in the main assembly room of the Royal Pump Rooms. This photograph is stamped 30 March 1968. (MWM)

Gentleman in a sedan chair being carried by two chairmen. The Regent Hotel is in the background. This appears to be part of the same Regency costume event as that in the preceding photograph and is also stamped 30 March 1968. (MWM)

A band playing in the Pump Room Gardens, c. 1965. The tower of St Peter's church is visible in the background. This photograph was used in the contemporary official guidebook to Leamington, which described the gardens as 'eight acres of open pleasure ground where bands play and fêtes are held'. (LSC)

The Theatre Royal, Regent Grove, c. 1890. Seating 1,000, this opened in October 1882 but generally ran at a loss. It was not until Charles Watson Mill took over the lease in 1916 that it became profitable. He presented pantomimes, circuses, plays and, especially, variety shows. After his death in 1933 the theatre was converted into the Regent Cinema. In the 1960s it became a bingo hall and then a store until it was demolished in the mid-1980s. (JV)

Servicemen outside the Regal Cinema, Portland Place, October 1946. The film showing, *Theirs is the Glory*, was a re-enactment of one of the turning points of the Second World War, the Battle of Arnhem. The cinema opened as a 'picture palace' in 1931 and is still in use today. (LSC)

Horse-drawn cart at Leamington May Day celebration, *c.* 1911. Edith Gaskin (later Mrs Banwell), then aged about eight, is sitting at the front of the cart.

Leamington College for Girls' choir, *c.* 1930. A note on the photograph states they were the winners of the Leamington Music Festival, which was held for many years in the New Bandstand and Pavilion in Jephson Gardens. The winners are named on the back of the photograph. Front row left to right: D. Warner, M. Davies, J. Gaston, J. Bastock. Back row: J. Ingram, M. Pugh, H. Berry, R. Gold, M. Harris, H. Jones, M. Franks, M. Plesker, G. Hinks, E. Plummer.

The Band of the Gold Coast Police played in the New Bandstand and Pavilion in Jephson Gardens as part of their tour of the United Kingdom in the 1940s. This photograph shows members of the band being met by the local constabulary; Mr T. Stenning, the bandmaster, is in the centre of the picture. The Gold Coast was a British colony when this photograph was taken but in 1957 achieved independence as Ghana. (LSC)

Left: Leamington-born Jennifer Chimes, who won the Miss Great Britain contest in 1955, wearing a dress made by the 'Ladies of Leamington'. The photograph is dedicated to family friends. She later married the comedian Max Wall. (MWM)

Below: The actor Geoffrey Hughes signing autographs when he came to switch on Leamington's Christmas lights, November 1980. He was then famous for his role as the scallywag Eddie Yeates in television's *Coronation Street*. He later became a regular in the television series *Keeping Up Appearances*, which often included scenes filmed in Leamington. (HEN)

seven

On Parade

The Parade in New Town epitomised spa elegance, providing a chance for wealthy visitors to parade in their fine clothes and meet other members of the social elite. The Parade kept its status even after Leamington had become primarily a residential town, some considering it so 'sacred' that 'working men and their wives should not walk up it'. Many of Leamington's most prestigious shops were on the Parade and its offshoots in Regent Street and Warwick Street. The Parade also connected to Victoria Terrace, which led to the longer established retail zones of the Old Town, including Bath Street and High Street. The grand Regency houses along the Parade and the other main streets could be easily adapted as shops by inserting large windows in the ground floors and fixing signs and awnings outside. The prestige of these retail zones was further emphasised by the presence of the town's principal hotels, especially the Regent Hotel on the Parade.

Looking south down the Parade. A sign on the right identifies the Bedford Stores of Burgis & Colbourne Ltd. The tracks and poles carrying overhead cables in the middle of the road are for the electric trams introduced in 1905. One of a series of postcards of Leamington published *c.* 1910. (JV)

Right: Advertisement for Burgis & Colbourne Ltd from a guidebook to Leamington published *c.* 1911. The Bedford Stores extended from the Parade to Bedford Street. The company was established in 1874 when grocers Charles Richard Burgis and James Colbourne formed a partnership. The business was purchased by the Army & Navy Stores Group in 1963, which ten years later was taken over by The House of Fraser Ltd. The latter still trades from the premises.

Below: The west side of the Parade opposite the Regent Hotel. The tallest of the buildings has painted on its side 'P.H. Woodward/Silk/Mercers/Drapers' – an advertisement for one of Leamington's best-known department stores. This photograph was used in the Royal Leamington Spa Development Plan (1947).

P.H. Woodward & Co. Ltd's department store on the corner of the Parade and Regent Street, *c.* 1930. This shop stood on the site previously occupied by the Upper Assembly Rooms. P.H. Woodward & Co. Ltd acquired it in 1908, expanding into adjoining premises in Regent Street in 1927. The interior was refurbished in 1938, the same year that saw the end of the system whereby staff 'lived in' the premises. The business continued to trade until May 2004 when the building was sold for redevelopment.

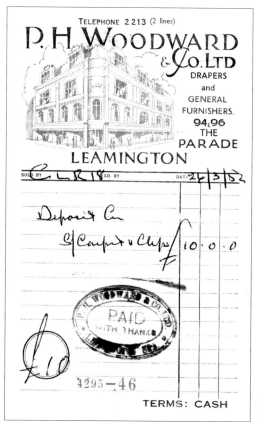

P.H. Woodward & Co. Ltd receipt dated 26 March 1952.

Harry Crawley's Tailor and Outfitter shop on the corner of Regent Street and the Parade, *c.* 1930. The floor above is occupied by a 'Hair Specialist' providing services including manicure, massage and the fashionable 'Marcel's Permanent Waving' for ladies' hair.

Marks & Spencer Ltd store on the Parade, *c.* 1930. After the company opened its first store in 1904 it gradually established others on the high streets of most major towns.

The west side of the Parade opposite Euston Place, 3 May 1960. The store closest to the camera, Bobby & Co. Ltd, is one of several well-known local businesses that have since disappeared from Leamington's high streets. (Edward Eves, Leamington)

Part of our up-to-date Café-Restaurant.

There is an air of distinction about Bobby's Fashion Salons which attracts attention.

You are cordially invited to visit the Store and inspect, at your leisure, the displays of all the latest styles in Coats, Gowns, Two-piece Ensembles, Costumes, Millinery, Gloves, Hosiery, Lingerie, etc.

Morning Coffee, Luncheons and Afternoon Teas are daintily served in the Café Restaurant. Music by Bobby's Orchestra 3.45 to 5.45.

BOBBY
& Co., Ltd.

THE PARADE :: LEAMINGTON SPA   TEL. 781-2

Advertisement for Bobby & Co. Ltd from a guidebook to Leamington published *c.* 1935. As well as the food and drink 'daintily served' in the café-restaurant, customers could listen to Bobby's Orchestra (visible in the background) playing from 3.45 p.m. to 5.45 p.m.

The west side of the Parade seen from the Town Hall, 4 March 1944. The Burton menswear shop (left) was one of many in British high streets at this period. St Peter's church is in the background; the block of buildings to the right has since been demolished and St Peter's car park erected on the site. (Leamington Borough Police)

Shops at 78 to 84 Warwick Street in the 1960s. These buildings are close to what is now the northern entrance into the Royal Priors shopping centre.

Bailey's furniture store, 73 Warwick Street, in the early twentieth century. By the 1960s Bailey's had replaced this with a more modern building on the same site.

Victoria Terrace was built in 1836–37 largely as houses (although the terrace included Victoria Pump Room & Baths by the Leam). Many of the premises later had their ground floors converted into shops, as seen in this postcard published around 1904. (HB&S)

The corner of Victoria Terrace and Spencer Street. This photograph was used in the Royal Leamington Spa Development Plan (1947).

The Regent Hotel on the Parade 'long enjoyed the reputation of being the finest hotel in the kingdom'. It was opened in August 1819 as the Williams' Hotel (named after its proprietor John Williams) but was renamed after the Prince Regent visited the following month. The young Princess Victoria and her mother stayed there in 1830. The Regent Hotel was owned by the Cridlan family from 1904 until it was closed in 1998 and later converted into a Travelodge. The photograph used for this postcard was also used in an advertisement for the hotel published around 1930.

The Clarendon Hotel on the corner of the Parade and Clarendon Avenue. This was built in 1830 to meet the need for a fine hotel at the northern end of the New Town. Advertisements often emphasised it was in 'the highest and healthiest part of the town'. The Clarendon Hotel closed in 1984 and has since been converted into apartments. The vehicles suggest this photograph was taken in the 1960s.

The Manor House Hotel on Avenue Road, c. 1892. This incorporated a house that had belonged to local landowner Matthew Wise. The building was converted into a hotel in 1847 and then became a school before reverting to a hotel. It is claimed that the first game of lawn tennis was played on the lawn in 1872. The hotel closed in 2004 for redevelopment as apartments. (FF&C)

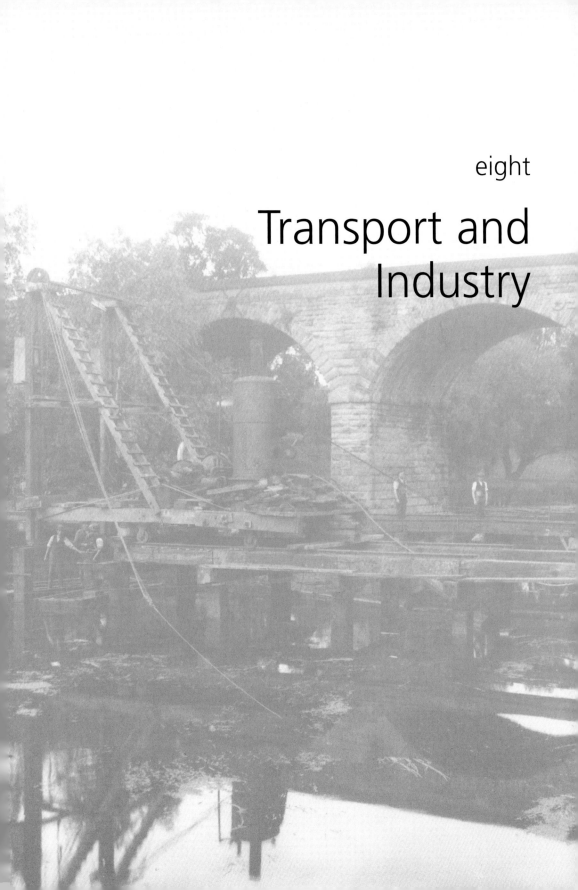

eight

Transport and Industry

Leamington's growth as a health spa and later as an industrial centre was assisted by its easy access to the Midlands transport network. The turnpike roads built in the eighteenth and earlier nineteenth centuries brought fast passenger and mail coaches to the growing resort, while the opening of the Warwick and Napton canal in 1799 provided cheap transport for goods. Later, beginning in 1844, Leamington was connected to the spreading railway system, providing fast and cheap long-distance transport for both goods and passengers. This helped Leamington cope with its decline as a spa resort by becoming a commuter town for Coventry and Birmingham, and by attracting new industries of its own. In the twentieth century the growth of the Midlands motor industry brought a number of companies to Leamington, notably the Ford Motor Co. and the Automotive Products Group. These remained major employers until recently.

LEAMINGTON TERMINUS.

Leamington's first railway station was on Rugby Road, Milverton. This print was published in the *Illustrated London News* on the day of the opening, 14 December 1844. It was the terminus of a branch line from Coventry that was later extended to a station on Leamington's Avenue Road.

Opposite above: Early rail travel could be hazardous. This image shows the bridge at Leek Wootton, near Leamington, after an accident on 11 June 1861. The bridge's cast-iron girders fractured and the locomotive and some empty coal wagons fell through. The driver, George Rowley, and the fireman, John Wade, were both killed.

Opposite below: Horse-drawn coach outside the Regent Hotel, *c.* 1900. At this time the railways provided most long distance transport but horse-drawn vehicles were vital for local journeys.

Above: Horse-drawn tramcar of the Leamington to Warwick tramway on Victoria Terrace, in front of All Saints' church. Trams like this had been used since the tramway opened on 21 November 1881. This photograph was taken after the shops in front of the church had been demolished in the mid-1890s but before work began on rebuilding the western end of the church in 1898. (FF&C)

In Loving Remembrance of the LEAMINGTON and WARWICK HORSE TRAMS,

Which succumbed on May 16th, 1905

to an Electric Shock. Aged 25 Years.

Let not ambition mock their useful toil,
Their homely joys, and destiny obscure.

Above: The introduction of electric-powered tramcars on 12 July 1905 is commemorated in this humorous postcard. The journey of just over three miles between Leamington and Warwick took around twenty minutes. The rattling and screeching of the electric trams as they travelled up and down the Parade annoyed some local people.

Right: Motorbuses began competing with trams on the Leamington to Warwick route as early as the summer of 1905. Competition became more severe after the end of the First World War and in the summer of 1930 the tramway finally closed. This advertisement for the Midland 'Red' company is from an official guidebook to Leamington *c.* 1930.

Opposite below: The replacement of horse-drawn trams by electric trams is commemorated in this postcard. The last horse-drawn tram service ran on 16 May 1905. The line was then reconstructed and a new electric powered tram service initiated two months later.

 Travel the Midland "RED" Way.

FREQUENT SERVICES TO ALL THE TOWNS and VILLAGES ROUND ABOUT.

USE ANYWHERE TICKETS, 5/-.
Available TUESDAYS, WEDNESDAYS, THURSDAYS and FRIDAYS.
A ONE-DAY PASS ALL OVER THE MIDLANDS.

:: DAILY TOURS ::
TO

Shakespeare Land, &c.
THROUGHOUT THE SEASON.

. *PRIVATE PARTIES.* .

Midland "Red" Vehicles available for Private Parties of any size or description.
Book early and reserve the date, settle details later.
Call at Local Office for Cheap Rates.

Local Office and Garage :
OLD WARWICK ROAD,   O. C. POWER,
LEAMINGTON.   Traffic Manager.
Tel. 194 Leamington.

Left: The bicycle became a popular form of private transport in the later nineteenth century. Jephson Gardens was the scene of an early gathering of cyclists when the 'Midland Bicycle Meet and Monstre Fete' was held on Whit Monday 14 May 1883. At this time the most widely used type was the 'penny-farthing' with one large and one small wheel.

Below: Cyclist crossing Victoria Bridge *c.* 1930. The introduction of mass-produced safety bicycles in the mid-1880s brought a new freedom to travel for both sexes, including the less well off.

Opposite above: Private motorcars began to appear on the roads from *c.* 1900, although at first only the very wealthy could afford them. A number of businesses were established locally to sell and service the new automobiles, including the Midland Autocar Co., founded by the Gibbs family in 1906. This shows their premises on Russell Street around 1910.

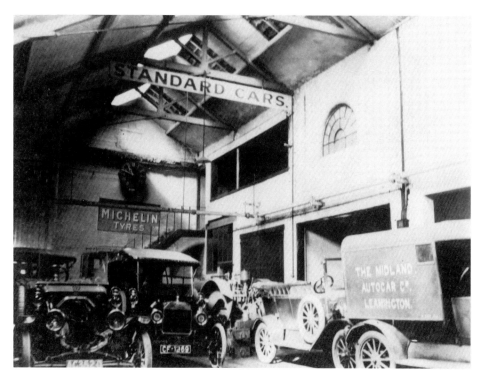

Below: The Midland Autocar Co. garage on Russell Street, *c.* 1965. The frontage of this building was rebuilt in the early 1970s by the Midland Autocar Co., which still occupies the premises. After the end of the Second World War, motorcycles and motorcars became affordable by increasing numbers of people, leading to the expansion of associated businesses.

This photograph of the Leamington Automobile Co. Ltd showroom on the Parade is dated 17 August 1959. (LSC)

The Regent Garage on the Parade, November 1976. The building, which earlier photographs show was in use as a garage by around 1930, was demolished in 1979. The site is now occupied by shops and offices.

Building the road bridge on Princes Drive, with the railway bridge in the background. The road bridge was built by A. Jackaman and Sons Ltd of Slough and the structural engineers were the Trussed Concrete Steel Co. Ltd. The bridge was opened in 1923.

Postcard showing the Mayor of Leamington greeting the Prince of Wales outside the Town Hall on the Parade, 1923. The Prince (later King Edward VIII) was in town to open Princes Drive bridge. (S.A. Mason)

Above: Oldham's Mill – also known as the Old Mill – on the river Leam. The Earl of Aylesford leased the mill to the Oldham family, who from 1832 to 1878 supplied Leamington with drinking water. The mill, with its tall chimney, floodgates and wall (used to create a public open swimming pool in 1869), was considered an eyesore by many people. Its demolition in 1899 allowed improvements to the course of the river and the laying out of Mill Gardens.

Left: The demolition of the chimney of Oldham's Mill, 29 June 1899. (EEL)

Above: The windmill on Tachbrook Road, *c.* 1892. The mill is probably that recorded as sold at auction by a Mr Bromwich on 29 October 1806. Its sails were removed in 1943 and the tower demolished in 1968. The Windmill Inn in the background is still a public house. (FF&C)

Right: Alderman Sidney Flavel (1847-1931) was the grandson of the founder of the Flavel company, best known for manufacturing cookers. The family sold the company in 1939 but it still manufactures cookers under the name Rangemaster. This photograph was taken in 1916. (EEL)

Above: The Ford Motor Co.'s Leamington Foundry on the Old Warwick Road. This was on the site of the foundry opened in the 1880s by the Imperial Stove Co. and taken over by the Flavel company in 1902. Ford's bought the foundry in 1939 and operated it until 2007. This photograph is stamped 16 September 1963.

Right: Visitors being shown around Ford Motor Co.'s Leamington Foundry. (LSC)

Opposite above: Sidney Flavel & Co. Ltd's transport department, Russell Street, *c.* 1965. The company's main factory was by the canal in south Leamington.

Opposite below: The Automotive Products factory on Tachbrook Road, built in 1931, was until recently one of Leamington's biggest employers. This photograph taken in 1948 shows Mrs Heather Hiley (front right) and her colleagues outside the factory's Block 7. Heather, seen here shortly after she joined the company as a clerk/typist, retired as the divisional manager's secretary in 1987.

"LET HOT WATER WORK FOR YOU"

Cleaning is a daily task—good reason, surely, to simplify such work, to avoid its drudgery. How ? *With hot water*—speedy, thorough cleanser. And how is hot water best obtained. *With gas*—cheap, clean, *unfailing* fuel ; heating water instantly, making no work. There's a gas water-heater to suit your home, to give you really hot water always for every household need.

Mr. G. A. Service on "Heat without Housework."

LEAMINGTON PRIORS GAS COMPANY,

SHOWROOMS: REGENT STREET, LEAMINGTON SPA.

32

Above: Leamington Gas Works seen from Ranelagh Terrace *c.* 1965. The gasholders in the background help explain why 'Gasworks Alley' is written on the back of this photograph. The gasworks on this site was established in 1838, replacing a smaller one whose origins go back to 1819. At first the coal needed to make the gas was delivered using the adjacent canal but later most came by railway. In the 1960s Leamington was converted to use natural gas from the North Sea. The gasworks was demolished in 1982. (T. Hull)

Left: The Leamington Priors Gas Co., which operated the gasworks on Ranelagh Terrace, had showrooms on Regent Street. The company was nationalised in 1949 and became part of West Midlands Gas. This advertisement is from the official guidebook to Leamington of around 1930.

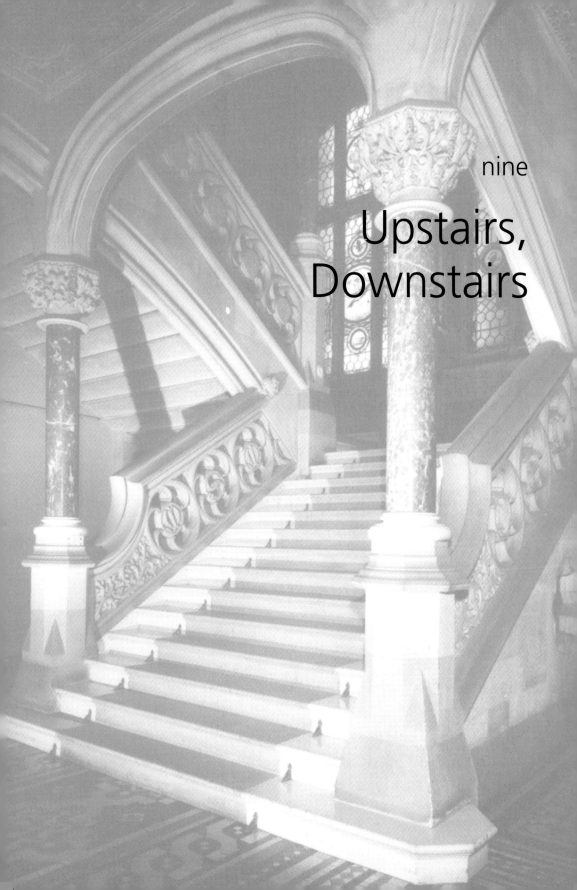

nine

Upstairs,
Downstairs

In the course of the nineteenth century Leamington developed a distinctly 'upstairs, downstairs' social structure, with a relatively large group of wealthy residents relying on services provided by a far more numerous population of servants and tradesmen. The 'large contingent of unoccupied residents who live more or less luxuriously upon their means' noted in a report of 1895 survived well into the twentieth century. There were also middle-class businessmen and professional people such as doctors, teachers and clergymen, together with their families. The division between well-off residents and the working classes was reflected in the housing. Behind the grand houses of the Regency terraces and the Victorian villas were the overcrowded dwellings of the poor. Their unhealthy streets and courts in the New Town were criticised in the *Leamington Spa Courier* as 'a sink-hole of crime and immorality' and it was equally as bad in parts of the Old Town. Slum clearance was underway by the 1920s but it was many years before the work was completed.

These cottages in Church Street in the Old Town must have been amongst Leamington's oldest surviving buildings when this photograph was taken around 1870. At this period photographic exposure times were fairly slow so the people must have remained still for some time. (BB)

Above: Frances Leigh Bellot (1820-1905) in the library of Moreton Lodge, Eastnor Grove, December 1900. The clutter of pictures and ornaments is typical of the grander houses of the late Victorian period.

Right: Rowland Edward Leyland Naylor (1851-1949) occupied Harrington House, Newbold Terrace, from 1904 to *c.* 1948. A man of considerable personal wealth, his staff included a coachman who wore a uniform and top hat. His wife was said to be 'delicate in health with hypersensitive hearing' – which may explain why he helped fund the replacement of the bandstand in Jephson Gardens with one further away from the house. (BB)

Bullock Bros   Leamington

Above: Harrington House shortly before it was demolished in 1967. The house was built in 1869 for Major Thomas Molyneux Seel but cost so much that he could never afford to live there. In the late 1940s Rowland Naylor bequeathed it to Leamington Corporation. During the Second World War it was used by the Czechoslovak Free Army, followed a few years later by the Warwickshire Civil Defence department. After the house was demolished the site was used to build the Royal Spa Centre. (WW)

Left: The main staircase in Harrington House. A member of the Warwickshire Civil Defence staff who worked there remembered it as 'a huge house with huge rooms and a beautiful staircase with a stained glass window at the top of the stairs.' The grounds contained stables, heated glasshouses and conservatories with palms and peaches. (WW)

Above: Lansdowne Circus, designed in the mid-1830s by the architect William Thomas, has eight pairs of semi-detached houses grouped around a private garden. This photograph was reproduced in the Royal Leamington Spa Development Plan (1947) with the caption 'Beautiful and still convenient small Regency Houses.'

Right: The American writer Nathaniel Hawthorne (1804-64) rented 10 Lansdowne Circus in the 1850s. His book *Our Old Home: A Series of English Sketches* (1863) described the circus as 'one of the cosiest nooks in England or in the world'.

Above: This terrace on Clarendon Square was built between 1829 and 1839. Each house had ample space for a wealthy family and half dozen or more live-in servants. The photograph is recorded as taken around 1968.

Left: Frank Gaskin with his family outside their home at 7 Russell Terrace, *c.* 1906. Frank also appears in the photograph of Bath Place Infants and Junior Schools in the next chapter.

Right: Frank and Melvina Gaskin with their daughter Edith, *c.* 1906. Edith, about two or three years old here, later became Mrs Edith Banwell.

Below: Covent Garden Market, which lay between Russell Street and Tavistock Street. The market established here in 1828 became surrounded by houses for the working classes. In the mid-nineteenth century the area was a badly drained, overcrowded slum. The market was disused by 1947 and the houses demolished shortly after this photograph was taken *c.* 1965.

Tavistock Street, *c.* 1965. Market Street, on the immediate left of the butcher's shop, led to the Covent Garden Market.

Working-class terraced houses in Althorpe Street in Old Town. This photograph was used in the Royal Leamington Spa Development Plan (1947) with the caption 'To live in these surroundings cannot produce good citizens or healthy children.' For many years one of the courts off Althorpe Street, although lined with houses, was used to dump cess waiting for disposal in the river Leam or later at Heathcote. Complaints from the residents were ignored.

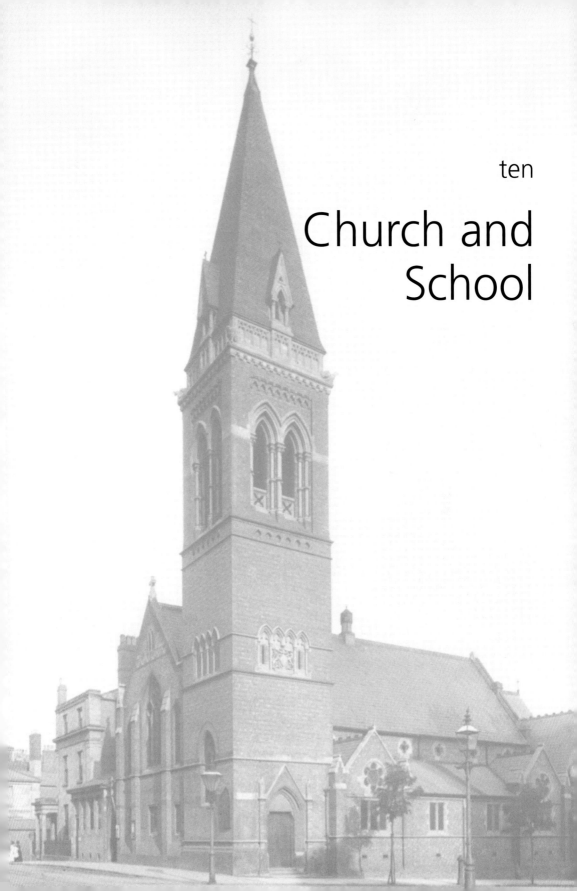

ten

Church and
School

Church and school were closely connected for much of the nineteenth century. At the beginning of the century Leamington's only place of worship was All Saints' parish church. As the population grew, the Anglicans founded new churches and chapels, as did the other denominations that settled in Leamington such as the nonconformists and the Roman Catholics. Many of these places of worship had associated schools for the poorer children. At first these were only open on Sundays but from the 1820s there were also day schools. This emerging schools system was increasingly regulated by the government, which eventually forced the Leamington Corporation to form a School Board in 1881. From 1903 the County Council became responsible for secondary education, later taking over the entire state school system in Warwickshire. One of the reasons Leamington Corporation had been reluctant to establish a School Board was that many of the wealthier residents educated their children at private schools and academies in the town. Some of these were fairly short-lived but others proved more enduring.

As Leamington grew it was necessary to extend All Saints' parish church to accommodate larger congregations. Building work was carried out on a number of occasions during the nineteenth century, the last begun in 1898 and completed in 1902. This photograph shows work in progress on the west bell tower in 1902. (EEL)

Above: The workmen employed on the extension of 1898–1902 outside All Saints' church. (EEL)

Below: All Saints' church could accommodate 1,500 worshippers when the extension was completed. This photograph of the nave is from a set of postcards of Leamington published *c.* 1904. (HB&S)

Christchurch, on Clarendon Avenue at the top of the Parade, was built in what has been unkindly called 'a pastrycook imitation of the Norman style'. It was opened in 1825 to meet the need for an Anglican church in the expanding New Town. Attendance declined in the twentieth century and the congregation moved to St Mark's church on Rugby Road in 1951. Christchurch was demolished in 1959.

The Catholic Chapel.

The classical style building on the left of this print was Leamington's first Roman Catholic chapel. Opened in 1828 on George Street, it was attended by Prince Louis Napoleon (later Emperor Napoleon III of France) during his stay in Leamington in 1838-39. It was replaced by a larger Roman Catholic church opened in Dormer Place in 1864.

The Congregational chapel opened in 1836 on Spencer Street – the chapel is recognisable by the portico with four columns. Four years later a school for boys was started in the basement, occupying a poorly lit, chilly space that they shared with the tombs of the dead! The chapel was the first building on Spencer Street, erected when it was still a rough track. This print is dated 2 November 1860.

St Mary's church, St Mary's Road *c.* 1892. This was opened in 1839 to meet the needs of the community that had sprung up as Leamington spread to the south-east. Its remoteness from the centre of town meant it was known for many years as 'St Mary's in the Fields'. (FF&C)

The Wesleyan Methodist chapel, Dale Street, opened in 1870. It could hold 1,300 people and replaced the smaller Wesleyan Chapel in Portland Street. The chapel shown here was demolished and a Methodist church built on the site in 1971. (Hosmer & Arthur, Leamington)

St Paul's church, Leicester Street, was built to serve the community developing on the north-east side of Leamington. The church was built in phases during 1873-75. It was dedicated for services on Ascension Day 1874 and consecrated with its own parish four years later. (JV)

Right: St Alban's church, on the corner of Warwick Street and Portland Street, opened in 1877 as St Michael's and All Angels. It was bought in 1881 by Dr Nicholson, formerly of Christchurch, who changed its name to St Alban's church. The tower was erected in 1887 to commemorate Queen Victoria's Jubilee. The church was demolished in 1968 and an office block known as St Alban's House now occupies the site. The tramway in the foreground appears to be for horse-drawn trams – in which case this photograph must have been taken before they were phased out in 1905. (JV)

Below: St Mark's church, Rugby Road, *c.* 1892. This was built to serve as the parish church of New Milverton. Opened in 1879, it was erected and endowed by Dame Frances Wheler and her brothers Charles Carus Wilson and Edward Carus Wilson. (FF&C)

The Sunday Schools' Centenary Celebration in Pump Room Gardens, 1 July 1880. The Sunday School Movement was established to provide schooling for poor children and the centenary was celebrated nationally. Leamington's first Sunday school was started around 1813 in the house of the curate of All Saints' church. Similar schools were founded later by other denominations that settled in Leamington. (C.W. Smartt, Leamington and Stratford-on-Avon)

The infant department of the National School in Bath Place, 1888. The school, established by All Saints' church and built with the help of a government grant, opened on 3 November 1859. (Martin & Tyler, Warwick)

Staff of the Bath Place Infants and Junior Schools, *c.*1910. Those shown include Mr Gameson, headmaster of the Junior School (centre front row) and Frank Gaskin (far left back row) who is seen with his family in the previous chapter.

Shrubland Street Girls' and Infants Board School, opened in 1884 by the Leamington School Board. The board was reluctant to spend money on education, building Shrubland Street School (which had places for 504 infants and 300 girls) for about half the national average cost per pupil. This picture was used in the Royal Leamington Spa Development Plan (1947) with a caption recommending that the school 'should be demolished at the earliest opportunity'.

The 'Municipal Schools & Public Library', Avenue Road, was officially opened in December 1902. In addition to the Public Library and a School of Art it housed the Technical School and the Secondary Day School for boys and girls. The schools largely shared staff, the director of the Technical School, Mr Mellows, becoming headmaster of the Secondary School. By 1922 the premises had become too cramped so the Leamington College for Boys moved to Binswood Avenue, leaving the Leamington College for Girls on Avenue Road. (WAL)

Miss Hunt and the prefects of Leamington College for Girls, May 1971. By this time the school was in premises on Cloister Way, occupied from 1959 to its closure in 1977. Those shown are: Front row, left to right: Anne Healy, June Engwald, Ana Kelly, Ruth Hope, Julia Onuferke (head girl), Miss Hunt, Gaynor Anderson and Carolyn Wallace (deputy head girls), Linda Freeman (senior prefect), Susan Dawson, Kathryn Nichol. Middle row, left to right: Rebecca Bayly, Victoria Rose, Jane Brotherton, Ghislaine Hunt, Margaret Tandy, Gertrude Morrissey, Gillian Bennett, Linda Moffat, Anita Langford, Valerie Reynolds. Back row, left to right: Marilyn Morton, Sally Pring, Stephanie Preston, Philippa Askew, Moira Lawson, Anne Reading, Barbara Rexstrew, Tina Webster. Behind the girls is a sculpture by Walter Ritchie, 'Three Aspects of a Young Girl's Education'. (MWM)

Leamington College, Binswood Avenue, c. 1900. This opened in 1848 as a private school 'for the sons of the nobility, clergy, and gentry' but had recurrent financial problems, finally closing in 1902. The building was then used by the Society of the Sacred Heart as a convent school until 1916, when it became a temporary wartime home to Dover College. The Leamington College for Boys was transferred from Avenue Road to this building in 1922. Since 1977 it has housed the sixth form of North Leamington School.

Schoolmasters and boys outside Leamington College, c. 1880. (Hetterville Briggs, Leamington)

ARNOLD LODGE, LEAMINGTON.

This is a good Boarding School for young ladies.

Beech Lawn Preparatory School.

♪ ♪ ♪

BEECH LAWN is a successful Preparatory School at which boys are prepared for entrance and scholarship examinations at the Public Schools and for the Royal Navy, by J. W. LIDDELL, Esq., M.A., and A. C. LAING, Esq.

Special attention is given to the younger boys. They are mainly in the charge of Mrs. LAING, B.A. (London), who also takes the instrumental music of the school.

The house, which is admirably adapted for a school, is large and airy, and stands in its own grounds in the higher part of the town and is only a few minutes' walk from the open country. There is a large and well-fitted gymnasium, where all boys undergo a regular course of physical training under a qualified instructor.

The playing fields consist of some seven acres within easy distance of the school, where cricket, football and hockey are played regularly. There is also a carpenters' shop, miniature rifle range and photographic dark-room. Swimming is taught in the summer term for which there are excellent facilities. The school also possesses a large lending library. Electric light has been installed throughout, and the drainage and sanitary appliances are of the most modern principle and certified by the County Medical Officer of Health to be thoroughly satisfactory in all respects. The domestic arrangements are under the direct superintendence of Miss Liddell who is assisted by an experienced Lady Matron. Recent successes include scholarships at Charterhouse and Westminster.

59

Above: Arnold Lodge School was founded in 1864 on what is now Kenilworth Road. Occupying converted private houses it took its name from Dr Arnold, the celebrated headmaster of Rugby School. It was originally for boys, although according to the sender of this postcard postmarked in 1904, 'This is a good Boarding School for young ladies'. By the 1930s it was being advertised as a Preparatory School for Boys.

Left: Beech Lawn Preparatory School, Warwick Street, occupied a large house that had belonged to Dr Henry Jephson. The school closed around 1936 and the building was demolished ten years later. The site was later used to build the present fire station. This advertisement is from a guidebook to Leamington published *c.* 1911.

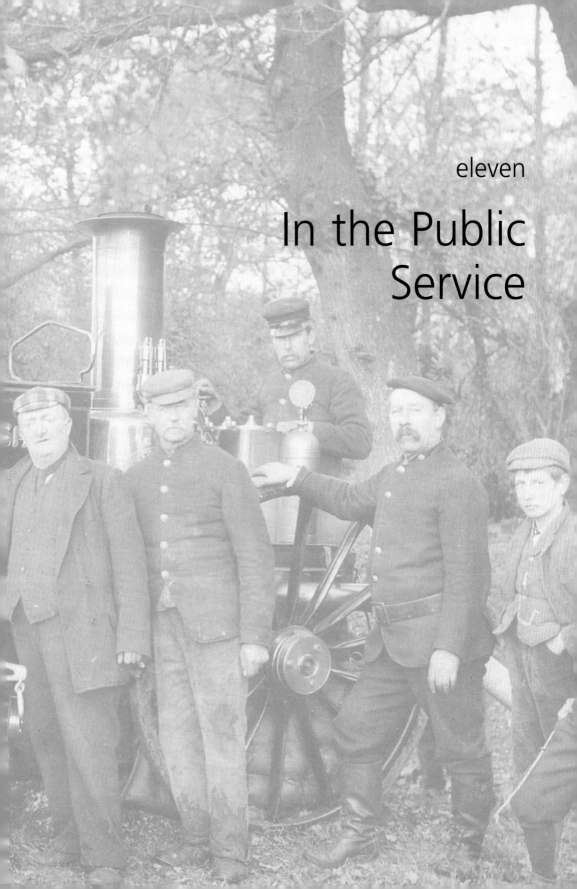

eleven

In the Public
Service

The growth of Leamington was underpinned by the development of public services, many organised through successive bodies responsible for local government. At the beginning of the nineteenth century the parish vestry of All Saints' church was the main body for local administration. In 1825 the vestry was joined by the Improvement Commissioners, responsible for 'Paving or Flagging, Lighting, Watching, Cleansing, Regulating and Improving the Town of Leamington Priors'. In 1852, after an outbreak of cholera caused by polluted drinking water, the Improvement Commissioners were replaced by a Board of Health. This initiated improvements to the water supply and sewage disposal. It also opened the first Public Library and purchased the Royal Pump Rooms. In 1875 Leamington achieved the status of a Borough with a Corporation consisting of a mayor, aldermen and councillors. This lasted until 1974, when some of Leamington Corporation's services were transferred to the newly formed Warwick District Council and the rest to the Warwickshire County Council.

The Town Hall on the Parade replaced an earlier one on the High Street. The new Town Hall was built by Leamington Corporation and opened in 1884 by the Mayor, Councillor Sidney Flavel. Its Renaissance-style architecture has been criticised as 'quite out of keeping with Leamington' but is now more widely appreciated. One of a series of postcards of Leamington produced c. 1904. (HB&S)

Right: Mr E. Bratt, 'the last Town Crier of Leamington Spa'. The bell was rung to draw crowds to his announcements about the town or parish.

Below: On 1 April 1947 the Leamington Borough Police force, then established for over a century, was amalgamated with the Warwickshire Constabulary. This photograph taken in 1948 shows the old borough force assembled on the steps of the police station on the High Street. This had served as Leamington's Town Hall from 1831 until the opening of the new Town Hall on the Parade in 1884. (LSC)

Left: Gas lamp outside the police station on the High Street, 1954. It was originally one of a pair of gas lamps standing outside the building. Since this photograph was taken the lamp has been removed, restored and placed on display in Leamington Spa Art Gallery & Museum. (W.G. Gibbons)

Below: Leamington Volunteer Fire Brigade, *c.* 1880. The fire brigade was formed in 1863. Its badge is visible on some of the uniforms.

Leamington Volunteer Fire Brigade crew with a steam powered fire pump, 1 January 1900. Later the same year the fire brigade was replaced by Leamington Police Fire Brigade, consisting of about twenty policemen enrolled as part-time firemen. (I.W. Findlow, Leamington)

During the Second World War, Leamington's Fire Brigade was incorporated into the National Fire Service. This photograph of a fire engine and crew was taken outside the Chandos Street fire station. In 1948 Leamington's fire service became part of the newly formed Warwickshire County Fire Brigade. (Thomas F. Holte)

Left: Free Public Library, 1858. The Local Board of Health had founded a free library for the town's poorer folk on 16 March 1857. One of the first public libraries in the Midlands, it opened in the Town Hall on the High Street but in November the following year was moved to these premises on the corner of Bath Street and Church Walk. Fifteen years later it had outgrown them and was moved to another building on Bath Street.

Below: An architect's impression and plan of the Free Library, School of Art and Technical School opened on Avenue Road on 12 December 1902. These were the first purpose built premises for the library, which had occupied part of the Town Hall on the Parade since 1885. Print published in *The Building News*, 22 November 1901.

Opposite above: Museum displays in the vestibule of the public library on Avenue Road. These were from a small museum that in 1915 was moved from the Town Hall to the library. This photograph was used in the *Report of the Borough Librarian and Curator*, 1922.

THE BUILDING NEWS. Nov. 22, 1901.

Borough of Royal Leamington Spa
Free Library, School of Art, and Technical School

J.L. Mitchell Bottomley
Architect

Below: Hanging the fourth Local Artists' Exhibition, January 1937. The exhibition was held in the Art Gallery extension added in 1928 to the public library on Avenue Road. The man with the pipe is probably the Borough Librarian and Curator, William Ewart Owen. (LSC)

The Bright Obelisk was erected in 1880 on Holly Walk to commemorate Alderman Henry Bright's 'untiring exertions' to ensure Leamington had a reliable supply of clean water. Until the 1870s the town's water had come from wells or the polluted river Leam. After a government inspector declared it unfit to drink Bright helped to persuade the local authority to build a new water works. The obelisk was funded through public subscription and this photograph includes a hand written dedication from Bright, dated 1881.

Alderman Henry Bright. As well as helping ensure Leamington had a supply of clean drinking water, Bright also supported improvements to the town's drainage system and the formation of a School Board. On 18 October 1882, as mayor he had the honour of laying the foundation stone for the new Town Hall on the Parade.

Right: Postman Frederick Smith, 1890. A note on the back of this photograph states that he 'retired on a good & well deserved pension' in November 1900, after forty-six years of service. (EEL)

Below: Leamington, like other British towns, was deeply affected by the First World War. Many local people were recruited into the armed forces and there were also sights like these horses on Greatheed Road in 1915. Someone has written on this postcard that '200 horses of the Ammunition Column Royal Field Artillery … were kept out in all weathers to harden them for the War. But many of them died.'

Field-Marshall Viscount Bernard Montgomery in his staff car 'Old Faithful' outside the Royal Pump Rooms, October 1947. Accompanying him in the car is Leamington's Mayor, Councillor Oswald Davidson. 'Monty's' achievements during the Second World War had made him a popular public figure. On this occasion he was in Leamington to receive the Honorary Freedom of the Borough.

Opposite above: Leamington's Civil Defence team on the balcony of the Town Hall, 25 September 1939. The Second World War had just begun so at this point the team was untested. This is reflected in the wry comment written on the photograph: 'The note is "Quiet Confidence!!"' Those shown are: sitting at front, left to right: Dr Gemore, Young, -?-, Sutcliffe. Standing at back, left to right: Smith, Sidwell, Clarke, Jones, Hellon, Mallinson. (LSC)

Right: Postcard showing the memorial for local people killed in action in the First World War. Dedicated 'TO OUR FALLEN HEROES', this was unveiled in Euston Place on 27 May 1922. The names of those who died during the Second World War and in subsequent conflicts have since been added. (Bryan)

Below: Leamington's Mayor, Councillor Oswald Davison, laying a wreath at the War Memorial, November 1946. (LSC)

Other local titles published by Tempus

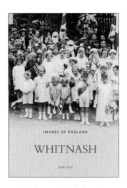

Whitnash

JEAN FIELD

Using over 190 archive images, this fascinating pictorial history charts the development of Whitnash from a rural village into a busy town on the edge of Royal Leamington Spa. Aspects of everyday life are featured, from schools and churches, shops and public houses, to leisure pursuits and celebrations – such as the Whitnash Carnival in 1950. Life in some of the surrounding villages, including Radford Semele, Bishop's Tachbrook and Chesterton, is also remembered.

978 0 7524 3512 1

Stratford-upon-Avon and Beyond

JOHN D. OLDFIELD

In this sparkling collection of over 200 old photographs and postcards, Stratford and the villages of three counties from the surrounding area are explored. From images of the streets and buildings, pubs and hotels, to the beauty of the river and surrounding countryside, and the development of the major insurance company and largest employer in the area – the NFU Mutual – all aspects of working and social life are chronicled here.

978 0 7524 0685 5

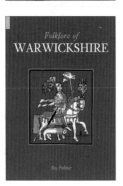

Folklore of Warwickshire

ROY PALMER

Situated in the very heart of England, Warwickshire is a county steeped in tradition, folklore and mythology. This is a fascinating illustrated study of folklore rooted firmly within the context of popular culture and history. Within its pages are tales of saints and sinners, sports and pastimes, fairs and wakes, folk song and balladry, as well at the passage rites of marriage, birth and death.

978 0 7524 3359 2

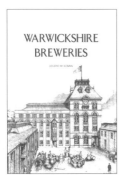

Warwickshire Breweries

JOSEPH MCKENNA

Complete with illustrations and listings of licensed premises, *Warwickshire Breweries* provides a fascinating insight into the history of brewing in this area. From the creation of a Common Brewery at Coventry in 1801 to the establishment of major forces such as Flowers of Stratford during the 1830s to the prominence of micro-breweries in the 1980s, this book charts the history of the county's licensed trade from humble beginnings to the present day.

978 0 7524 3755 2

If you are interested in purchasing other books published by Tempus, or in case you have difficulty finding any Tempus books in your local bookshop, you can also place orders directly through our website

www.tempus-publishing.com